Clovis Crawfish and Simeon Suce-Fleur

Mary Alice Fontenot

Clovis Crawfish and Simeon Suce-Fleur

Illustrated by Scott R. Blazek

PELICAN PUBLISHING COMPANY

GRETNA 1990

Library of Congress Cataloging-in-Publication Data

Fontenot, Mary Alice.
    Clovis Crawfish and Simeon Suce-Fleur / Mary Alice Fontenot ;
illustrated by Scott R. Blazek.
    Summary: Clovis Crawfish rallies his animal neighbors in the
Louisiana bayou when his new friend, a handsome hummingbird, gets
caught in a cold snap.
    ISBN 0-88289-751-9
    [1. Crayfish—Fiction. 2. Hummingbirds—Fiction. 3. Animals-
-Fiction. 4. Bayous—Fiction. 5. Louisiana—Fiction.] I. Blazek,
Scott R., ill. II. Title. III. Series: Fontenot, Mary Alice.
Clovis Crawfish series.
PZ7.F73575Clhb 1990
[E]—dc20   9-35370
                                                          CIP
                                                           AC

Printed in Hong Kong

Published by Pelican Publishing Company, Inc.
1101 Monroe Street, Gretna, Louisiana 70053

For G. D. ("Chief") Barras and Yvonne LaHood,
Parrain *and* Marraine
of Simeon Suce-Fleur

It was like springtime in south Louisiana. There were patches of green clover here and there in the brown, frostbitten grasses, and it was cozy-warm in the sunshine.

Clovis Crawfish had spent all of the winter down in the bottom of the hole under his mudhouse. He was very tired of staying inside.

Clovis crawled out of the round hole in the middle of his mudhouse. He unfurled his whiskers and flexed his big, sharp claws.

Up on a willow branch, Rosalie Redbird twittered. Her mate, Rouseb Redbird, was down on the ground pecking at some weed seeds.

Clovis spied Christophe Cricket peeking out from under the root of the big oak tree. *"Eh, là-bas,* Christophe!" said Clovis. "Hello over there. Come on out. *Voici le printemps!"* which means "Springtime is here!" in French.

Christophe began to chirp this song:

Vive le Printemps

Music by Jeanne and Robert C. Gilmore

Vive le prin-temps, le beau prin-temps, en-core le chaud s'approche. La

p'tite gre-nouille elle chante, chante, chante, en-core les jours se ré-chauffent.

Translation:

Hail to the spring, the beautiful spring, again warm weather draws near.
The little frog sings, sings, sings, again the days grow warmer.

Lizette Lizard crawled down the tree trunk. *"Bonjour,* Clovis! *Bonjour,* Christophe!" said Lizette. "I saw a wild violet blooming this morning, and there are lots of yellow butter-weeds in the marsh!"

"And the buds on the willow tree are round and green!" said Rouseb Redbird.

"Then it's time to start building our summer home," said Rosalie Redbird. She flew off to fetch some twigs for her nest.

Clovis looked around for his other warm-weather friends. Nowhere could he see René Rainfrog, Gaston Grasshopper, or Josette June Bug.

"Maybe it's not spring time yet," said Clovis. "I'm going out in the swamp to find out. I'll ask Henri Hibou, if he hasn't gone to sleep yet." *Henri Hibou* is the way to say Henry Owl in French.

Clovis crawled fast, fast.

He saw a tiny *suce-fleur*, which means hummingbird in Cajun-French. It was shiny green, with a ruby-red throat, and it flew by so fast Clovis couldn't even see its wings move. It went straight to a wild azalea flower and began to suck the honey. It flew up and down, then backward and forward, its long bill darting in and out of each bloom.

"*Bonjour!*" said Clovis.

"Bonjour!" answered the tiny bird. "My name is Simeon Suce-Fleur. Do you know where I can find some spider-web threads for my nest?"

Clovis wiggled his whiskers. He pointed with his big claw. "Right over there by my mudhouse," he said. "Old Simone Spider used to live there, but I had to chase her away so she wouldn't trap my small friends."

"Merci," said Simeon Suce-Fleur, as he flew away as fast as he had come.

Clovis looked all around. The wild fern fronds were curling up out of the ground, lavender violets were blooming under the cypress trees, and the air was warm and balmy.

And there was Henri Hibou, looking outside from inside his hollow tree house, his eyes half-closed.

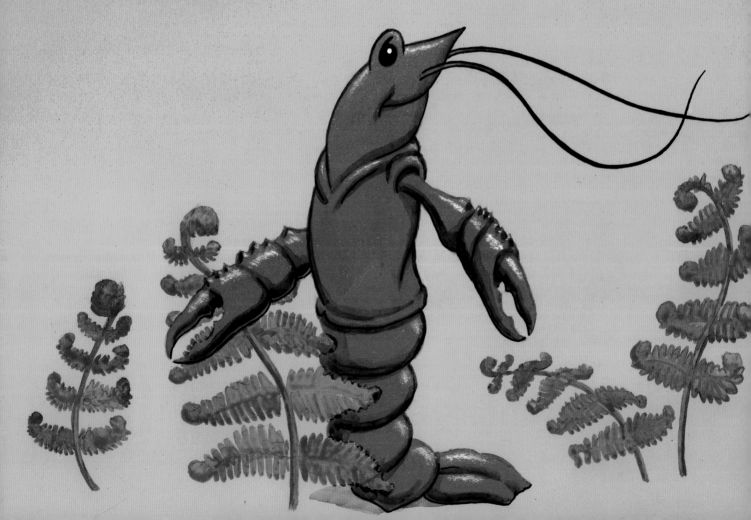

"*Eh, là-bas*, Henri!" shouted Clovis. "Is it springtime?"

Henri Hibou rolled his head around and winked one of his round eyes. "*Pas encore*," he answered, which means "Not yet" in French.

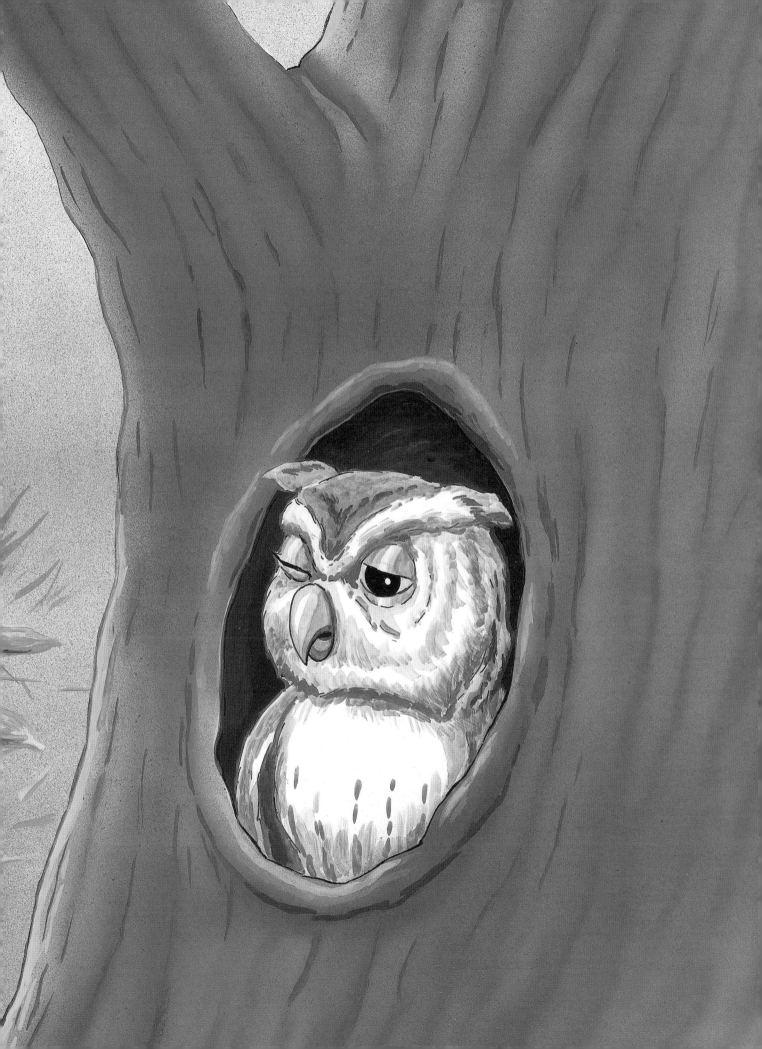

Clovis was disappointed. He backed up and turned around.

The sky had turned gray and an icy wind crackled the bare tree branches. A little something—soft, white, and very cold—fell on Clovis's hard shell.

"What's that?" Clovis asked in wonder.

"That's a snowflake," said Henri Hibou. "Watch out! Here comes a whole bunch of them!"

Clovis had never seen snowflakes. He stared at the pretty feathery flakes falling, falling, and covering everything with a cold white blanket.

Clovis shivered. He crawled fast, fast until he got near his mudhouse on the bayou bank.

Then he found Simeon Suce-Fleur. The poor little hummingbird was on the ground, half-frozen, his body and wings covered with a blanket of snowflakes.

"Help! Hurry!" Clovis called. Lizette Lizard and Christophe Cricket had disappeared, but Rouseb Redbird came flying in.

"What can we do, Clovis?" asked Rouseb Redbird.

"Find Andrew Armadillo," said Clovis. "Hurry!"

Rouseb Redbird flew off, his feathers bright red against the flurry of white snowflakes.

Andrew Armadillo came loping up so fast he almost fell in the bayou.

"Vite! Vite!" cried Clovis. "Quick, quick, dig a hole. It's warmer under the ground, and maybe Simeon Suce-Fleur will thaw out. Hurry!"

Andrew went to work, the sharp claws on his front paws scattering dirt, leaves, and snowflakes.

He helped Clovis drag the little frozen bird to the hole,
then they gently covered him with dirt and leaves.

The next day the sunshine was so warm it melted all the snow. Clovis hurried to the hole where Simeon Suce-Fleur was buried. One tiny green wing was sticking out from the dirt and old leaves.

"*Viens ici,* Lizette!" Clovis called. Lizette helped Clovis pull Simeon Suce-Fleur free of the damp dirt and leaves. The little bird opened his eyes, shook his feathers, then flew up and lit on top of Clovis's mudhouse.

"*Merci, mes amis!*" said Simeon, which means "Thanks, my friends." He spread his wings and away he flew. "*Mais oui,*" said Clovis Crawfish. "*Vive le printemps!*"

PRONUNCIATION GUIDE

French	English	Approximate English Pronunciation
eh, là-bas	hey, over there	*ey, lah-bah*
voici le printemps	spring is here	*voi-see ler prenh-taw*
vive le beau printemps	hail to the beautiful spring	*veeve ler bo prenh-taw*
encore	again	*onh-kor*
le chaud	heat	*ler show*
s'approche	approaches	*sah-prosh*
la p'tite grenouille	little frog	*lah pteet grin-oo-ee*
elle chante	it sings	*el shaunt*
les jours	the days	*lay zhoor*
réchauffent	gets warm again	*ray-shauf*
bonjour	hello	*bonh-zhoor*
Henri Hibou	Henry Owl	*onh-ree e-boo*
suce-fleur	flower-sucker	*seuce-flurr*
merci	thanks	*mare-see*
pas encore	not yet	*pah zonh-kor*
vite	quick	*veet*
viens ici	come here	*vee-yanh zee-see*
mes amis	my friends	*mays ah-mee*